IT IS WHAT IT IS, WHAT IS IT

Praise for IT IS WHAT IT IS, WHAT IS IT

"In IT IS WHAT IT IS, WHAT IS IT, we are never sure whether we are the subject or object of desire as language slips around us, revealing and occluding our most intimate scenes: our triumphs, our losses, our deaths. When the world suddenly becomes smaller, tighter, and the words fail, Spencer Butt reminds us that no matter what 'we're just trying to get better at embracing the unknown / like John Lithgow hugging sasquatch in *Harry and the Hendersons*'. Warning: these poems will pull the rug out, then catch you before your head hits the floor."

~ Jason Christie, author of *Cursed Objects*

"There is a scene in Kurosawa's film *The Seven Samurai* where they audition warriors. One man beckons a prospective warrior inside the building for a chat while hiding next to the entrance is another man with a heavy stick to strike him. They believe the best warrior should have instincts proving they can deal with such a surprise. One fails and gets hit, one reacts so quickly he doesn't get hit, but the best just before entering, stops and suddenly looks confused. Then calls out to the man beckoning him inside, why is there another man standing where I can't see him, holding a stick? That's the difference between everyone I know who says they are a poet and Spencer Butt. I can prove it; randomly open this book anywhere."

~ Bob Wiseman, author of *Music Lessons*

"In IT IS WHAT IT IS, WHAT IS IT, pop culture references fly by faster than the Springfield Monorail in this brilliant look at fatherhood, loneliness and existential angst. Spencer Butt speaks to us in a 'remorse code' that soars with a punk rock rhythm trying to decipher the heartache of remaining hopeful in what might seem like end times. These poems shove a mirror in the face of a world that refuses to see itself flailing away in a desperate attempt to connect. These poems demand we pay attention to the pain and the loss of living, even if it's only to mark our own passing. IT IS WHAT IT IS, WHAT IS IT is the power chord we need to listen to right now. Plug in, turn it up and read these words aloud."

~ RC Weslowski, author of *My Soft Response to the Wars*

IT IS WHAT IT IS, WHAT IS IT

Poems

SPENCER BUTT

[N₁ O₂ N₁]
CANADA

Publisher's note: This book is a work of fiction. Names, characters, places and incidents are either the product of the author's imagination or are used fictitiously, and any resemblance to actual persons living or dead is entirely coincidental.

Library and Archives Canada Cataloguing in Publication

Title: It is what it is, what is it : poems / Spencer Butt.

Names: Butt, Spencer, 1982- author.

Identifiers: Canadiana 20220494460 | ISBN 9781989689493 (softcover)

Subjects: LCGFT: Poetry.

Classification: LCC PS8603.U866 I8 2023 | DDC C811/.6—dc23

Printed and bound in Canada on 100% recycled paper.

Now Or Never Publishing
901, 163 Street
Surrey, British Columbia
Canada V4A 9T8

nonpublishing.com
Fighting Words.

We gratefully acknowledge the support of the Canada Council for the Arts and the British Columbia Arts Council for our publishing program.

for Henrik

COOL NEW FACE

is that me?
am i that?
is that a reflection, a portrait, a selfie, or a doppelganger?
a cheap halloween costume?
am i based on a true story?
am i reality tv or a mockumentary?
do i look at the camera? am i the narrator?!
am i having an out of body experience?
am i dead?!
have i been dead the whole time?

is that me?
the dumpster on fire
        kids roasting hotdogs and marshmallows
        in my fiery open mouth?
is that me?
        the milkcrate lawn chair on a fire escape
        the ankles and knees that crack like dry lips
        the buzz cut camouflage on bald dudes
am i that anxiety attack lullabye?
that ghoul with high cholesterol?
that always tired george costanza
        in a stretched out funhouse mirror?

is that me?
do you see me too?
that looks like me,
checking my bank account on my phone in the grocery store,
calling my anti-depressants my roommates
        to make heavy times lighter
and wearing out all of the crotches
        on all of my favourite jeans
        in the same week.
i could swear the phonebooks of my palms

and remote viewer tea leaves
and magic the gathering tarot cards
said it was going to be different.
tapped broken telephones whispering white picket fences
and happy endings
and less stress
and dryer eyed moments of clarity
broken telephones that talk in tongues
like satan wants to french my brain
broken watches with the uncontrollable tick of turrets
broken sweat walking to the store to buy fruit punch
because it's pretend healthy

am i that?
that raccoon dressed up like weekend at bernie's?
that guy on an ebike dressed like sons of anarchy?
that late night club sandwich pita from 7/11
that you bought so you don't go home alone?
am i the dead beat of a broken snare drum?
the flat tires on a bike painted white
chained to the streetlamp at a scary intersection?
the excuses made to stay home
and little spoon with your couch?

is that me?
dead bird in a puddle?
is that person eating
a family sized bag of doritos on the bus me?
are they too confident to be me?
do i WISH that was me?
is that the dream?
is this setting goals?
is this too far fetched?
am i setting the bar too high

to be that person eating the doritos?
can i be that?
can the guy from those community college commercials
yell at me through my tv
until i stand up straight
            and start making more eye contact
            and stop grinding my teeth in my sleep?
can i copy and paste a new face onto myself
that's a bit more welcoming and a bit less welcome mat?
can i even afford a cool new face?
            in this economy?

is that me?
is that me in the corner?
is that me in the spot...light, losing my religion?
am i just plagiarizing r.e.m. now?
            when the fuck did i start doing this?!
have i been plagiarizing r.e.m. this whole time?!
can i stop any time that i want to?
can i?
can i be that and not this?
can i inch towards instead of running back?
can i pause it for a bit while i catch my breath?
when is the "enough" in "enough is enough"?
should i set my alarm?
do i say when?
do you?
who does?
this is not rhetorical!
this is not a test!
when do i stop asking permission?
why so many questions and apologies?

is that me?
is that my signature shadow, shape, and slouch?
is this the series finale?
the curtain call?
the grim reaper's pink slip?
the grand "clean out your desk" in the sky?
fingers crossed,
i'm just gonna close my eyes for a bit
and wish myself to sleep.

I STILL BELIEVE IN BIGFOOT

in this scenario we're going to make it
        the fires have been put out
in this scenario it's hot but early july hot,
        not dante's inferno wet t-shirt contest hot
in this scenario we're all sleeping fine
        and backs don't ache
        and eyeballs don't jump out windows
in this scenario
        i am haunted inside too
in this scenario
        my outer goth and inner hermit
        are locked in mad maxian missionary position
in this scenario
        this is the best kind of hard it's ever been
in this scenario
        we don't need to lie on the floor to ease the pain
or unwind
or have booze dropped off
        like an orphan in a picnic basket in front of a fire station
in this scenario
        we smoke weed for fun and not to dull
        the knife is far too murdery in this scenario
        and can leave you needing stitches
        if you're within 6 feet of it

in this scenario we're brave enough
to wear white shirts or not wear hats
we've never lied about our height or weight
        or diet or general level of fitness
in this scenario
we're fine with how we look and sound and walk
and dress and sweat and cry and laugh and sleep
in this scenario
        i saw my all favourite artists   live

before they died of a disease
an addiction
a killing themselves
in this scenario
that last part doesn't sound like
i made these stranger's deaths about me
and my idiot slug needs
in another possible scenario
i didn't need to make a joke about that to feel comfortable

in this scenario
our neighbours have never made a peep
through the walls
we've never been traumatized
in this scenario
none of our loved ones have ever had track marks
or gone through withdrawal
and therapy is free
and personal days aren't embarrassing to take at work
in this scenario
everything works out the way you want it to
concerts start on time and finish by 11pm
there's a vaccine for hangovers
there's a stretch that cures grief
your kid has never felt scared
and you've always felt safe
like your guardian angel is the color a kryptonite lock
or the shape of rottweiler
or smells like the honey that killer bees make
and we don't have to keep making up fantasy worlds

A LAGOON

what are we packing?
            what do we take with us?
            what do we want and what are we stuck with?
            what's a luxury item
            and what suitcase do burdens fit in?
how heavy
            how heavy and the wheels are broken
            so we drag and hurt our everythings

what goes in first?
            soft things shield delicate things
what are we bringing?
            what will we miss and what is essential
            what do we think we need but just cling to obsessively
what's stuck?
            what do we leave behind when
            there is no more room
and will we wish we had chosen differently
            once we get there

what bags and baggage
backpacks that will have us trapped on our backs
            if we tip
            when we fall
too much weight
the weighting is killing us
is this a hipsack full of broken watches
and cuckoo clocks with birds flown south?
why do this?
where are the canned goods?
what doesn't rot?
what won't spoil? where is the spoiler alert?
what about a blanket?
what about an invisibility cloak

what is it about going outside that seems lousy
          seems like work
          seems made up
          and dangerous
          and too spooky
what do we have in our luggage to defend ourselves
          what would make a good weapon?

have we thought about the carrying?
          we carry so much with us
          we're not very strong
our muscles are mostly vestigial
          a limp tail
          an internal organ acting like it's supposed to be there
          sneaking past the stanchions into the v.i.p. area
          playing it as cool as possible
          which is not very cool
          standing in the corner and observing
          like an anthropologist in a dumb band shirt
          the third eye on a primitive makeshift lizard
we could get stronger
          if we practice
lift this bagage over and over again
act like it's lighter than it is
so we don't scare off the inner bellhop of a kindly stranger
          so people don't think we're struggling with our stuff
          so people don't get out of our way
          and instead make a point to get into our space
          like a lonely rocket ship
          or determined viruses
but it's tough
the bags feel like they're full of pure gravity
a suitcase of slumps
a duffle bag of fight or flight magazines

the pages torn or stuck together
our favourite songs crashing around inside a shoulder bag
and some make us crumple
and some make us tall
and some make us sad
and some make us
wish we had packed a time machine
instead of old calendars
and and half melted,
long extinguished birthday candles
wax twisting with old icing

next time we'll make a better checklist
plan the trip better
ask for more of a heads up
from the air raid sirens and catastrophes
we'll start drafting that letter
and see if anybody wants to publish it
once we get there

SLOW V. STEADY

it took me forever
    to get my shit together
and even then
    through the building
    the construction
    the hammering and nailing
    early morning banging when you need a break
    letting the foundation harden
    the blueprints and step by steps
so many other things fell apart.

the illusion
    this rad magic
    this slim fit witchcraft painted onto a husky curse
    these sick spells beat up sneakers
this progress that others might commend
    or even aspire and lust for
    longing for the short term
this place i'm at now
    a final (for now) destination
    where the maps nap
    where i'm pausing the game
to walk around and stretch my legs
    to shop or eat or wander
some people
might see this one spot
and have no idea about the route i took
think this looks very nice
    very scenic
    no quicksand in sight
    the pavement looks fresh underfoot
and they think they'd want to visit
book that trip
    look into a timeshare
but the cost was so great
that i'll be forever in debt

NICER THAN I THOUGHT

can i fuck that tractor?
can i fuck your pickup truck?
may i 69 your hay bailer
          or make out with the bowling alley?
can i hold hands with those snowmobiles or dirt bikes,
ridden to school and parked in their own parking lot?
am i flirting with the convenience store?
wanna hang out in that one parking lot?
          in that one pizza place?
                    behind the portables?
                              at the quarry?
wanna vandalize while wearing promise rings?
wanna skinny dip in a creek
before it's part of that new golf course?

i have erotic dreams of the city
and public transit and stores open past six and on sundays.
i fawn over malls and draw hearts
around the movie theaters i sketch on my binder.
who will i love when the big box stores empty your shell?
how much will i miss you after i've moved away
and don't make it back for your funeral?

SELF ASSURANCE IN THE QUARANTEENAGE

at least i haven't seen my loved ones in a while
        thank god
        (you pick which one)
that's a plus of this all
i wish i had the putrid yawn of a subway creep
bum rushing my nostrils
to remind myself why i love this city so much

i have kicked my excessive hugging addiction to the curb
no more physical warmth from another human,
        that's what this housecoat is for
        that's what these sweatpants do
i also don't feel the need to ever leave the city anymore
this quarantine is like a giant
        spiritual
        full body
        nicotine patch
        unfucking up my life
last year was shit (the bad kind)
        and i was going to finally turn shit
        (see: stuff)
        around this year
and it's so much easier when i can't leave my house
        or feel terrified about going to buy groceries
thank the heavens that i maxed out my credit card
        right before the entire earth got sick
        otherwise i could just order supplies online
i'd be so ticked about that right now
        so blessed that it's not an option for me
        i should start a social media account about this
        tell me about your depression on my onlyfans

i always thought i would miss the pigeons but i don't
i didn't take photos of them
        on the ledge of the window that

my desk is next to at the office
before we went home for good
(see: forever)
i haven't filmed them and given them names
and jobs and back stories
i didn't get emotional the day i saw their eggs hatch
or when i thought the parents
weren't coming back that one time
i wasn't totally shell shocked when i realized their nest
was basically just made out of garbage and their own waste
i don't wonder how they are
and doodle them while listening to sad music

i'm glad i don't feel like i'm not growing or learning stuff
i hated that general vibe, you know
i'm glad i'm getting better with my words
i wish people were around to play pranks on me
and lie
i feel fine
i feel fine with the dimming of light friendships

i'm glad i can't hear you at our favourite bar
that i'm not nodding
and smiling over the very loud music
because i just like the way your face moves
when you're telling a story
i'm glad i can't go for a stroll on a weekend morning
to grab freshly baked croissants
and eat them in the park
thank fuck i'm not worried about
certain specific friends right now
because their immune systems
are as fragile as moth wings
in these uncertain times
i am positive this will all be over soon

TAKE WUT U NEED

take what you need
this is for everyone
take it and feel better
            well i didn't think you needed that much
            no
            no no
            it's fine
i'm just a little surprised at the amount of
            no
            i meant it

take what you need
your needs are your needs
i wouldn't have said it if i didn't mean it
it is, after all, kind to offer
yes
i am smiling
this is not baring teeth
this is friendly
I have read about friendly and i am sure of it
            wikipedia
            well i trust it
ok i will practice
            yes in front of a mirror
i don't know how often but i will
i mean
i'm very busy these days
suuuuuuupes biz
but
i'll work on incorporating it into my usual routines
take that for what you will
take it

take what you need
you can barely handle that much
you're a greedy t-rex
but no
    nope
    there are no rules as to how much
    i did that on purpose
there was intent
there was a reason
    when i first said this
there was good will
    notice that
    take notes about that and tell people about that
and a mission statement
there was a goal
a point that is now very pointy
    spear like
    maybe too sharp
    maybe i should top it with a cork so we don't
    jab ourselves

oh space is what you need?
    got it
oh time?
oh space and time?
    got it
oh and silence
    got it
and pitch black
    got it
oh and some white noise
    but i thought you said silence
oh white noise is different
    got it

i’m dumb
take it
take what you need
take it to your safe haven
and take your time
take two
take care

IT IS WHAT IT IS, WHAT IS IT

oof!
what a lungblower
very winded
        a deep suck and oversized exhale
stretched out
        to dizziness
        to a little galaxy in your eyeballs
        to polkadot cataracts
        to a head on the moon
floating migraines
        with helium aneurysms
it is what it is, what is it

yikes to this
oh bother
        oh no
        oh my goodness
what an unwanted tingling
        what static skinjobs
        what slimy auras
        what undulating birthmarks
allergic reactions full speed ahead
a rash of maybes
        put some ointment on that!
and pulsing eye twitches learning remorse code
when you should be sleeping
        you gotta wake up early tomorrow
it is what it is, what is it

smelling burnt out
the perfume of detroit techno
the potpourri of repetition
the bathroom air freshener of a million yesterdays
a tincture of deja vus

photocopying essential oils
the peppermint does nothing
but cause a paper jam
and it floods
god damns break
and we pray for a lifejacket
or flutter board
or a log
so we can go with the flow
instead of floating face down
our backs turned to the sun
manic depressive loch ness monsters
as the fish tanks in our chests
swell to haunted bouncy castles
one last sigh as we sink
it is what it is, what is it

THE WAKE

that's your alarm clock
not the one
on your phone
　　　　on your nightstand
　　　　that wakes you up
the one that sets something off
　　　　a starting pistol loaded with hollow points

that's your alarm clock
that says it's time
　　　　but then asks what a clock is
that makes you move
　　　　like an eviction
　　　　or bed bugs
　　　　or a breakup

that's your alarm clock
　　　　not the one mandated by work
　　　　not the seed planted by bank accounts
this one won't water that
this one will make you thirsty

WITHOUTS

i'm not talking as much
            and it's good
my jaw is on vacation
            and it's good
my brain is fine
            it's never better than fine
            so fine is fine
            and it's good

silence as camouflage
as a spell
as a panic room
            with cool movies and books and snacks and weed
            a tree fort made out of an armored car
            a pillow fort with bulletproof cushions
when the bombs drop it'll be loud
            and then bright
            and then quiet

electronic music plays at a murmur decibel
the copycat footstep
            and an echocardiogram on ecstasy
my favourite song starts with what sounds like a nightclub
            full of people
            talk over the music
and it's nice to hear

EIGHT HOURS

so glad
i hurt my back sleeping
this memory foam booby trap
double crossing tie dye sheets
voodoo doll pillows
so glad that i am made of sensitive glass and puddy

feel it
up and down in your ribs
            and your gut keeps the pace
            and it's not fast
there's motion
it's moving
consistently and without thought
this is keeping time
this is a pendulum exercise
this is rest

TWO KINDS OF PILLS

in the distance
            a plane whirr
            beige hum
and softly closer
cars on new asphalt
            and a stroll or bicycle wind
            and velvet chit chat
            on the sidewalk
            100 meters away
            4 floors down

in the close up
            some ambient orchestras
wince as a motorcycle screams by
the bed
            gentle and paying attention
holds the chalk outline of my blob body
even after i migrate to the couch
            or to the fridge
            or to the bathroom
            or to the balcony
            or gone

inside
            my skeleton is packed with dumb things
            (mostly remorse and regret)

and apparently my heart isn't great
            (i'm on pills for that)
and my brain isn't great either
            (so i'm pills for that too)

what vitamins do lunatics take
        is there a supplement that will make you psychic
        a protein powder for remote viewers
        electrolytes for astral projection
what does it taste like
        I hope the answer is "banana medicine"
i hope the capsules aren't too big
i don't wanna choke
        and i insist on dry swallowing for no reason
like a total psycho
like all the water dried up
this could be my big break

ON MUTE

i used to only write
five page rants
and now i write very small whispers
but both can feel like a lot
depending on the volume

everything is an interruption these days
distractions swarming
          buzzing
          stinging

everything wants to stop you from achieving greatness
          from reaching genius
from grabbing at awards
like those plexiglass booths
          with the fan in the floor that blows money up
and you catch it or something
it's in movies and tv shows
you know what i mean
          and can picture it more clearly than you can
          your postal code or a close friend's date of birth

everything exists as something just out of sight
everything is shiny
and blindingly sparkly

i used to only write poetry
but then i heard the real money is in prose
          if only i could focus for more than
          a handful of stanzas i'd be so rich
          swan dive into gold coins loaded
          rubies in my teeth instead of blood when i floss
every novel is a best seller
when the grass is astroturf and you're obsessed with green

ISOLATION AS A FORM OF BONDING

like tall grass
            without buildings
            and maybe with a forest or just a fence at the horizon
            and with light blue up there
            and a few clouds moving faster than you're walking
            and open hands in the tall grass
a rippling surrogate wind
            making the tips dance
            palm to the future

it's different in the nostrils
here
things smell different
noses welcome it differently
chests do push up differently
something is less cumbersome about it
            it's a bit easier
            to breathe deeply and however you want
            when you can pretend
            you're the only person on earth for a little bit

just long enough
to let your lungs heal
            and tongue lean
            and lips soften
just long enough for your posture to hover
            and your eyes to glide
it's good to be whatever this is
whenever we can

BE SAFER

it rusts
        s l o w l y
        incompletely
        in increments
little specks of shimmer
        when facing the sun just right
still blind
but you can do without your sight for a second
when the sharp glow hits
eyes open like a scream
the pupil stretching
        we all see in spandex

over
        and over
        and over
braiding
flips in time
somersaulting through the void
cartwheel with legs barely up
        but take a video anyway
lots of tumbles
        in the inky forever
of the gap between your bed and the wall

you spent
over one hundred dollars
        that you don't have
in a crystal store
        that you didn't need to go into
        across town
your house
the wizard's cave
the fortune teller's overpriced one bedroom apartment

in an overrated city
the temple of debt
a coven of geeks
now featuring neat rocks that clutter your bookshelf
    the one near the window
at sunset
and if the stylish witches that were working the cash register
    the ones you instantly idolized
hadn't given you little print outs with each gem
then you'd have already forgotten what their names were
    or what part of your mortal coil
    they were protecting
then they'd be nothing more than monolithic marbles
instead they're paperweights of the occult
    and celestial bookends

CULTIVATING MASS

i'm dad
i'm daddy and dadda
said in happy and sad
and mad and annoyed and sleepy voices
i'm the property of my son
            his name's written on my tag
i am his best friend
well like, he's mine so i say i'm his
so it's less sad but who knows where
he's at with the ranking system
and all those hot wheels and stuffed animals
and maybe i don't really want to see
which number's next to my name
how about this,
if he wants
i am his best friend
and a guardian and a climbing wall
i am the builder of castles
            and band-aid applier
            and book reader
i am the snack maker
i am the hand holder and storyteller
i am a clown
            i love being the clown
his laugh is my favourite song
i am ecstatic even when exhausted

parts of my body hurt
like they didn't used to
            (shoulders, lower back, brain, knees, arms, heart)
i am fatigued and so very lucky
i am what i always wanted but never had
i am making the most of this
            and growing i hope

and learning i hope
and adapting i hope
and getting better i hope

i am the pupil of the eyes of my favourite teacher
i am soft piano
or light rain on a window when he needs to dream
i am a villain when he doesn't want to go to bed
i am always worried about him when i can't see him
and always happy when i can
i am trying to lead by example
and i am evolving based on his reactions
and books
and his mom
who is the parent that i have posters of on my wall
like a sports hero
she dunks on fools
and runs fast as trains
and knocks out bullies
and is a master chef even when she orders pizza
the pentagram star i draw in the margins
of my high school science homework
like the logos of rad bands that i wish i was in

i wear less scary heavy metal shirts these days
because he's scared of them
he was born of encyclopedia and comic book
of athlete and indoor kid
of cryptozoology and skeptic
of buffy and of vampire
and i won the lottery
he's my cash for life jackpot
i am proud to the point of tears
daily

i am a wreck with love
but the pieces of me that fall apart
look like a kind of avant garde sculpture
            so i am making it work

i am lucky and never forget it
i'm doing pushups these days
because he's getting to heavy for me to carry around
            but i love carrying him around
            and i hate doing anything physical
            so like
            i hope he knows that's huge
            even if my muscles aren't

SANCTUARY

it's a set of weighted eyelids
your vision is a little blurry
maybe the corner is blurrier than the middle
you question
your glasses prescription
before realizing
you just need
to go to bed

no amount of zzzzs seems to
fully fix it
            you're sure you read somewhere that it should
maybe you're low on iron
or need to exercise more
or maybe you're just bored a lot
it's probably a buffet of ennui
and if not even that very good name for a goth band
can get you motivated
then something is wrong

it feels good to lie down
but maybe clean first
so when you scan the room
            the debris free floor
with vaseline on the camera lens
it all feels more calm

if the apartment feels like it just
took a bath and can now zone out
then why can't the
art goblin that lives inside of it

RISK//REWARD

i am an emotional daredevil
        how fresh! how fun!
watch me swim through a sea of depression
        no water wings
only to dive back in when it should be done
        pool noodle in hand
so that i can sponge up more misery

lights camera action
i am the evil knievel
        of grown men who exclusively listen to the cure
behold
        the marvelous sight of a business casual
        joe dirt impersonator
as he lights himself on fire
and then tries to put it out with a bucket of gasoline
how wonderful!
how spectacular!

i am the johnny knoxville of heartache and break
        watch as i incase myself in a solid block of ice
        in a wildly misguided attempt at self care
this is both death and logic defying
        two for one thrills and chills

i am the jackie chan of eating chips for dinner in bed
i am the harry houdini of falling too far in love
i am the flying wallendas of social anxiety
no one person should be able to cry so much
without dying of dehydration
and yet, here, before your very bloodshot eyes is
a real-life homer simpson
        cannonball hitting me in the breadbasket
        in slow motion

as i drink orange gatorade
        because it's the colour of a real juice
        (he must do crossfit!)
lift the hand painted circus tent flap,
adorned with cartoonish portraits of freaks
a big canvas mockup of me in victorian animal pelts
        that kind of looks like a khaki shrek
        who smokes too much weed
and witness these astonishing feats for yourself!

SHHHHHHHHUT UP

we think you are great
absolutely tip top
amazing
beautiful
wonderful to be around
so truly interesting
and as long as we never actually speak
we can keep that story running in our heads
so please stay the fuck away from us
you magical unicorn who could be the one
but we can't risk learning otherwise
so if you even so much as ask us for the time
we will blow a gasket
you incredible one of a kind probably special gem
you presumed needle in a haystack
you maybe diamond in whatever the fuck a rough is

we are cartoon wolves
with a red carpet tongues
over the *you* we have constructed
based off of social media
or meeting you once a couple of years ago
or seeing you across a room a few times
this is the greatest love story ever known
you are rose in titanic and we are…
...the door
and jack is…
...i don't know who
maybe like a mutual friend or an uber driver
and the ocean is like
better, healthier life choices
but honestly it's just you, kate winslet the actor
and us
the floating door

against the world
how romantic is that
          (please tell us)
how truly delusionally sweet of us
to throw that metaphor together on the spot
what a non-weird
and definitely sensual thing to say
          you're welcome
person whose name we don't know
and do not really want to find out
what if it's the same name as somebody we already hate
and then they would cling to you
          like a needy burr
          or grass stained freckles
we can't risk that imperfection
          the stakes are too high!
we can't wait to never put ourselves out there
our lunchboxes are crowded butterfly nets
          just thinking about how nice it is avoiding you
and that distance
keeps us as warm as the fireplace channel
          and we just really need that right now.

THE TRUTH ABOUT GHOSTS

my son is 4
and starting to understand death
            no
            good god
            that doesn't mean i'm threatening him
there's a cemetery near our house
it's big and beautiful and quiet and we walk through it
and he's learning to ride a bike on it's pathways
and he's curious

telling a kid about death is tricky and scary
because you don't want to trick them or scare them
when i took him to the museum
i explained that some cultures have very ornate burial rites
            and sarcophagi
then we went to a bookstore
the clerk was showing us a book about halloween
and asked him if he liked pumpkins
he exclaimed excitedly
            NO! I LIKE COFFINS AND TRAINS!
            (i was so proud i nearly fainted)

when he asks if ghosts are real i say no
so he won't have nightmares
but i think
i lived in a haunted house in my 20s
            and the lying doesn't feel great
and the minute he can read the spines
of all the books about
the paranormal that line our shelves
he's gonna flip

NO MAPS ALLOWED

we wanna get lost with you
we wanna have no idea
stumble through the dark
run with eyes closed
            scissors in mouth
breath held delicately like hugging a sick child
feet that dance and skip
            like they're tangoing over trip wires
            mamboing around landmines

we wanna get lost with you
run in increasingly artistic circles
            a spirograph hedge maze
            paint splatter connect the dots
let the repetition lull us into a dream come true
we wanna get lost with you
and shred all the maps before we take off
            nobody needs to find us
because together we feel
both invincible and invisible
            just how we like it

we wanna get lost with you
            and go full specter
we've never felt more alive than doing nothing with you
we wanna walk through walls with you
until we get swallowed up
by the bright pink velvet void of happiness
we wanna get lost with you
and smile instead of asking for directions
            lock eyes instead of looking at street signs
            helix our fingers and sweaty palms
            in lieu of hitchhiking
we don't need star charts

because we think you're out of this fuckin' world
we don't need a compass
because we got magnets in our blood
when our hearts get racing
grinning idiots in jet packs
drooling in love
breaking sound barriers and boring plans just to hang out
when our hearts go hummingbird
        and DNA pumps like microscopic pistons
        those compasses are gonna spin anyways
        arrows everywhere
        like the climax of an old western movie

we wanna get lost with you
because we've found without you is trash
        missing you like y'all
we find ourselves not ourselves
we're looking for clues we've already tagged and bagged
we wanna get lost with you over and over again
we wanna get lost with you
because we're not really lost just taking the long route
        making our own path
        stopping whenever we want

we wanna get lost with you
        because we've been lost on our own
        and it's dreadful
there's no real lost with you
        you anchor
        you quest marker
        you beautiful intuition
we wanna get lost with you
and figure it out forever
we wanna get lost with you

and grow like we have a fucked up pituitary gland
our love is andre the giant in his prime
        massive and with weird teeth
        and a french accent and a drinking problem
        but larger than life in the best way

we wanna get lost with you and be here all along
we wanna get lost with you
and find new stuff along the way
we wanna not know and be pleasantly surprised
yes right here and now is cool too
        we're not not trying to smash light bulbs
        or pinch flames just for the sake of it
we're just trying to get better at embracing the unknown
like john lithgow hugging sasquatch
in harry and the hendersons
        and editing out the scene where he yells at him
        because we're too breakable
let us be your swamp ape and we will show you the world.

YES GOOD

it's great when it shuts the fuck up
when it's quiet
when muted
when it whistles fast wind
it's great when it hums a blackhole
when it echoes the night
when the power goes out in its teeth
when the verbs sleep
            and the words abandon ship

it's great when it's still
it's greater still
when it moves so slowly that you'd think it wasn't
small signs of life when you stare really closely
tiny hopes when you let your eyes unfocus
it's great when it's calm
when vaccinated for motion sickness
when stable
thoughts cradle instead of crush

in this moment
            in the here and now
when the bouncers won't let the ifs and maybes in
when the second hand rubs your back
you delete the bad luck from your contacts
because you get what you give
            and they just give you panic pains
            and you don't have gift receipts for them
            so you can't trade them for rational thought
            and you can't afford the added drain
work is a bummer
rent is due
groceries are expensive
you went on a medium date this week

that cost you a large bill
in this moment
you find deep breaths
in this moment you find
a lack of bullshit
and worry
in this moment you're ok

ON THE INSIDE LOOKING OUT

this terrarium isn't all bad
        this drywall fish tank
        this low-rise lookout
        this brick-and-mortar crow's nest
pointed north
we watch
the go trains and via rails
run back and forth on the bridge a block away
late night rapscallions stumbling drunk
towards the sketchy bar on the corner
because the alcohol shook their etch-a-sketch brains

what was it like before
we moved like angry uhauls
fast cars with tracy chapman murals airbrushed on the side
nifty fact blurbs blurred
as empty cubes scurry to and from empty houses
alpha and omega rentals

this biodome is fine for now
we buy house plants
to try to fill and root ourselves with yes's
and no no's like voldemort writing inspirational quotes
this bird cage will do
this is not the forever
charlize theron got her start in
children of the corn iii: urban harvest
and she turned out ok
so we can
guzzle vitamin d pills
tag people in instagram bullshit
do exercises and tell the world
now i am become couch
for a little bit

for the love of our sick friends and our grandparents
and we too will be ok

put some cumin in your coffee
a pretend a yoga master said it'll make
          everything better
even though it tastes like fucking trash
and you're just pretending it doesn't
you white college student with dreadlocks
          and the slipknot logo in henna

this cyberpunk afterlife
this outerspace toolshed
this real-life rear window
could be a lot worse
          could be terrible
          could literally be a coffin
we're just temporary unabomber recluses
in long distance relationships with reality tv shows
let's take breaths as big as our lungs will allow
and cross all of the fingers that
this mindset doesn't get canceled after one season

THIS IS A TEST

it's not easy
to fake it
            this much
            this often
            cheeks ache

people don't buy it
when you have a bad poker face
            when you never learned how to play poker anyways
when you'd rather play magic cards
and escape just for a little bit
            instead of work on yourself

it's not that simple
it's not copy and paste
            cut and dry
there's a lot more than two sides
            it's a d20 with a multitude of possibilities
in the no man's land of best and worst case scenarios
it's walking up hill and breaking a sweat way too fast
            like, you're alarmingly out of shape
            like a "when the fuck did this happen?!" panting
and there's a very good chance
you're not wearing the right shoes for this
            let's blame the shoes and use covid as backup

how do we break this down
            without having a full breakdown
            without getting stranded
            because we never bothered to learn
            how to take care of our own engines
            or even change our tires
what do we do
to convince the moment not to sprint into the sunset

        don't spook it
to be here for longer than the click of a second hand
        right fucking now

how are we supposed to pump the breaks
when we're obsessed with cutting them
meditation is dumb
        your brain doesn't care
        how much ram dass you listen to
        says, "fuck off, hippie"
        when you try to force the serenity
        to tame the sheets on the clothesline
        when they just want to writhe in a the wind

hands constantly refreshing phones
        with eyes that hit windows
        like flies with somewhere to be
out there is too much most of the time
        but can't live up to our
        unrealistic expectations when we visit
if it's always something else then it's never our fault
        right?
if it's always too late
then we don't need to get started
if it's too much work
then we can always finish it tomorrow

who comes up with these bad ideas
where's the editor
how do we get our own private focus group
        that isn't just friends or family
        or a therapist we can't afford
        (but also can't not afford)
guilt and grief

dumped onto a conference room table
strangers with clipboards taking notes
and we're peeping toms behind a two way mirror
figuring out which details of ourselves
should get cut
before airdropping our dating profiles to masses

RIGHT NOW

in this
ambling day
pink clouded
pastel dusk

in this
sweatshirt and hat
running shoes
steam dream

in this
bus gusts
shuffle garbage and
ripple loose clothing

in this
flailing trance
peripheral theme song
with the gps turned off

in this
intentionally located
where you need to be
even if it's not where you want to be

DEMO VEHICLE

this isn't really
how its supposed to be
the first few drafts
looked nothing like this
the brainstorming
the storyboards
it's not how we pictured it
it's a mess but it works
            how well it works
            has yet to be seen

this wasn't supposed to
turn out this way
not even the same ballpark as this
            was it even baseball?
it wasn't supposed to go
anywhere near this
and we're making it work
            (kind of)
forcing it to show up
and if you enjoy your job
you'll never work a day in your life
            (i work around the clock)

there are moments
where the sun shines so brightly
            the colors pop
            it's a warm and a beautiful painting
            the kind you'd see in an expensive doctors office
            or a fancy bathroom in a ritzy restaurant
and those times
make it worth it

when the little things
equal
the best moment
of your day
and you journal it
          or better yet
write a poem and it gets into a cool magazine
maybe that's your bonus

WE'LL SEE

i'll buy pretzels and a tall can of 99 cent iced tea
and hide
i will flop around
i will wish i had bought
            something sweet to chase the salty
i might stand on the balcony
            or i might not
i might stand at the window
and consider getting some fresh air
            or i might not
i might open the window next to my bed and lie on it
            (my bed, not the window or the window ledge either)
with eye envelopes shut
and imagine i'm walking
i will almost certainly stay up too late
on the first night of my days off
and throw off my sleeping patterns for days
            the trail is lost
i will shower and get dressed
            but for lunch, not breakfast
movies might come over
books will pop by
music or a video game might call
but i'm fine if none of this
or if some of this
or if modified versions of this happen
or don't

RISE ABOVE & FALL BELOW

what if we all autumn
all of the people
what if we don't have any idea what a lot
of dead people actually is
or who would run the power plants
            turn the water on
            tuck us in
how long were the dinosaurs here for?
how long did we live next door to neanderthals?
how sad were we
when they stopped coming out to play?

what a rad blip we are
the here and now of a comma
            the lasting impression of khaki pants
            a very memorable footnote

how will the next civilization
jigsaw puzzle our bones together
will we look like us when they see us?
would we recognize us?
will we have feathers or scales or fur or tails?
what tools of ours will make it into museums?
should our descendants
make sure to delete our browser history?

BETTERER

it's an improvement
it's medium better
it's ok ok
it's growing by standing up straight instead of hunching
it's the illusion of height
it's a drawing of a band-aid
and the embrace of a tight sweatshirt

it's so so
it's meh
me? i'm meh
i would rather be meh than mal

it's disgusting but you can stomach it
if you hold your breath it's fine
you're blue in the face with stubborness
but the color looks good on you

it's is a mystery
a miracle
a mirage
a manic episode
        where you write what you at first think are
        really impressive poems
        but then you get emotional
        when you read them back a couple of days later
        so you'll never show them to anyone
a moment of mania
a monday night messiah after a sunday scary

it's going to be something
        not great
        but like, goodish
it doesn't get great

great is functionally extinct
but it's going
it is stirring
it is movement

TUGS OF WAR

my brain got the best of me
        got away from me
        got into a car accident
        got thrown in jail
        got abducted by aliens
        got in over our head

my brain got carried away
        by vultures or ferrymen that thought it was dead
        or seagulls that thought it was part of a hotdog
        or a little wind that thought it was a crumpled up leaf
        or a kid who thought it was a cat's eye marble

my brain got offers it couldn't refuse
        and it didn't read the fine print
        or was just acting like it could read in the first place
        or quit and then came back the next day
        and acted like it didn't
        or mumbles "do over" when it's sleeping

my brain keeps fucking up for inspiration
        or says it saw a movie that it didn't
        or loves a book it never heard of
        feigns knowing the words to a song
                and moves its lips like a bad dub
        acts like it feels alright even when it's unwell

my brain worries about relapsing
        and the drugs from the doctor help but not enough
        and the drugs that i smoke
        run their fingers through my hair
        when i need to calm down
and the spiraling i'm addicted to
        is bound to cut my head off like a buzz saw
and won't stop sending nudes to panic attacks

THE BOAT

the boat
had wandered too far from the water
and it's stuck
and it's covered in mud
and feels fat
        feels heavier than it used to
        than it should
the propeller is reaching tippy toe
to the bottom
        hoping it's a little wet
looking to slide its foot
into a damp
comfort blanket

the boat is confused
wonders how it fucked up this bad
feels like it fell asleep and things were rocky but buoyant
and now it's so different
        and awful
        and trapped in this different awful

it happens to boats
sometimes a big wave or a hurricane
will chase a boat or push it around
and then the boat heads for higher ground like a jedi
before it realizes that boats can't be jedi's
and that the closest this boat will ever get
        is being a dead blue whale
        huge and magnificent
        but ultimately coffin shaped driftwood
boats don't learn or grow they just are
they are expensive and make people throw up
you have fun until the boat sinks
or money gets tight

or decisions are made
and the boat attempts to evolve and grow legs
to find a better spot
and then the boat is covered in mud
and stationary
and watches the ocean roll
as it pretends it did this on purpose

COBWEBS IN LOW LIGHT

will the change be gradual
            or immediate
a shock to our system
a jolt or fright
will we feel the kick
            what's the impact like

will we know it's happened
are we expected to wake up one day
and just be the change
are we getting sucked into dumb motivational posters
and dumber instagram influencers
            is change a vacuum or a canon?

will it cover us
            like warm bath water
            or
            cobwebs in low light
will parts be left out
            frozen ankles in pants that are too short
            sweatshirt cuffs that creep up forearms
            under the forcefield of a winter coat

if it isn't immediate
will we fight it
will we try to hold on to the used to be
            for reasons we're not sure of
            for reasons we're embarrassed to say
            or scared to admit
for just because or safety
is uncertainty the same thing as fear
when it comes to change
this is not rhetorical
we need to know

before the change takes place
            grabs a hold of us
just in case it makes it a bit easier

COMING SOON

hubba hubba catastrophe
            am I right?
            am i?
            lmk
this apocalypse is something else
a very cutting edge pompeii

this ain't your grandpa's twister
revolving lungs gasping in the spin cycle
            these houses flip and make money
            these tsunami's spritz and smell of epsom salts
            this building's on fire but i was getting chilly anyway

the blizzard is forcing a squint
and everything moves with caution
            tiny slide steps with eyes on toes
unsure of where the ice is but knowing it's there
            somewhere
and will it be the kind of ice
that you fall through and drown because of
or the type that makes cars dance
or the type you get frozen in
and scientists in the future will try to thaw you for a zoo

as long as the earth swallows us
            one big gulp
            no stress no mess
that's all that really matters
            am i right?
            am i?
            lmk
this apocalypse is really taking its sweet ass time
a fashionably late mount saint helens

DISTANT RELATIONS

it's not impossible
but if it feels like it
if impossible and it have the same texture
        the same the grit
if they both get jammed up under your fingernails
you take them both with you
as your hands pendulum when you walk
        or shelter in pockets
        or greet people with shakes or tremors
if impossible and it are there when you give
        a thumbs up and the middle finger
if they love each other very much
then they're the same

they share a bed
        maybe a mailing address
        maybe a last name
        maybe two last names hyphenated
        or combined into a new word
        a word search of same
        jumbled twins
two different types of play doh
squeezed together and stuffed back into
one plastic jar
with a pop top

your it and impossible dont need
        to be someone else's
they can be yours
heavy snowflakes
        unique in trauma
        and experiences
        and tension
        and strain

you don't need to compare two things
this isn't a child's paper restaurant menu
"spot the difference" game
or a simple maze with no crayons to find your way out
this is a mirror
or a polaroid
this is yours and it can feel like whatever you want
    role play the texture
    the grit
    the sighs with dirty fingernails

NOW LOADING

it shouldn't
have taken us this long to realize
that it's ok to be satisfied
but it did

it shouldn't have taken us x years
to look up the definition of "content"
but here we are
          creased spine of a miriam-webster
flabbergasted looks on our faces

it's not a
buy stuff to fill the void
          (well, it is sometimes)
but it's always been
a need to be bigger and better
and you can grow until custom clothes are required
without ever feeling like
you're in the right skin underneath it all

sometimes
it's rooted in poverty
the effect of growing up with bills getting cut off
can squeeze the life out you
with its phantom limbs

sometimes
it's a side effect of low self-esteem or mental illness
          why not both?
          the curse of buy one get one free
          wonder twins with identical destructive traits

there's no neat way
neither clean nor interesting
to fix it
or speed it up
no power tool for your brain
no game genie cheat codes
and neither
the drugs you buy in a store nor from a pal
work that well
and talking about it
to a psychiatrist or a pal
helps a little
but words get sore and veins dry up
and you're always gonna be you
to a certain extent

it feels more like a fluke
a hail mary epiphane
a lucky lightning strike
in the middle of a shitstorm
and even when it's sort of too late
the sudden boost is nice
maybe your engine can get jump started again
and even though it took you a while
the tortoise wearing your passport as a backpack
will still make it to the finish line
and get a pretty ribbon for participating

WHERE DOES IT ALL GO

why the fuck do i have
so
Much
stuff

everywhere stuff
covered in dust stuff
in big bins that i don't look at stuff
stuff that i used to collect but now just takes up space
stuff that i thought would be worth something
but now i don't want money
i just want less stuff

my closet has too much stuff
i bought a bed frame that could fit boxes under it to house stuff
why am i building subdivisions for stuff
when my natural instinct is to be a slumlord to stuff
to evict stuff
get rid of it
out on the curb
donate some stuff
and then dumpster the rest of the stuff

stuff needs to respect my fucking boundaries
for real, stuff
give me some breathing room, stuff
stuff needs to stop hitting on me
toxic stuff
stuff with benefits
that only benefits stuff

my apartment isn't small
but it is when i factor in the extra roommate that is stuff
stuff that doesn't pay rent

        or its share of the bills
stuff that says "hashtag clutter" when it takes a selfie
        tags junk
        @'s hoarders
        hopes for a retweet
stuff is so desperate and gross

stuff overwhelms me
why is there so much stuff on my nightstand
        on my dresser
what is this stuff
        stuff i've never seen before
        stuff that manipulates and causes dependency
am i addicted to stuff?
        can i stick a patch to my upper bicep
        so that i don't need stuff anymore
        maybe chew a gum
        maybe a hypnosis
stuff is a leech on my bank account
and a nuisance when i'm trying to find stuff
that i actually want and need

i purge stuff regularly
        (i feel a lot better when i do)
sick of stuffs bullshit
sick of stepping over stuff
        or stuff falling over
        because stuff wasn't stacked properly
there's no love in the architecture of stuff
        just lazy jengas and
        the tetris of "i'll find a better spot for this stuff later"
maybe it's a chair or a table that stuff has colonized
        and you'd love that land back
and when you take it

you have such big plans
        for this plot
        for this spot
        for a stuff free life
and i bet some other stuff would look great there

NOT RHETORICAL

what's it like
to be about to leave your apartment
and then you hear a neighbour in the hallway
but you just step out of your safehouse anyway

what's it like
to not wait inside
    ear to the door
    listening to murmurs
    not trying to decipher the words
    but just waiting for them to dissipate
    proceeded by the sound of a door shutting

what's it like to get invited to something
and think
    well this should be fun
to look forward to being highly social
to not plan an excuse to leave early
or not go at all

what's it like to be chill
instead of always tense
to wake up and not immediately start thinking
    planning
    strategizing
    being tired again

what's it like
to just exist
to not default to the glow of an app
to not want desperately to be absorbed by the background
or wish for a minor natural disaster to save you

THINGS YOU'LL WANT TO DO AFTER READING THIS POEM

lie down
kill me
ask me what's wrong
high five me
ring my neck
gouge out your eyes
wish you had never read this poem
write a better poem
write a poem that isn't as good as this poem
        (and ruin your day)
laugh
        (for pleasure)
laugh
        (psychotically)
cry
cry more than usual
barf
make love to dynamite
apologize to somebody
        (finally)
feel better
feel better
        (the other meaning)
take a walk around your house
        your block
        your neighbourhood
take some good inhales
        and maybe a couple bad ones
take it one day at a time
        even if all of the days are running towards you
        full tilt
take a nap and botch your sleep tonight
think that not all poetry is stupid
        even if you're not sure what side of the argument

this poem lands on
wonder if this is a poem
decide it's not a poem
drop this book off at a used book store
buy this same book back in a couple of weeks
(from the same used book store)
out of pity
or nostalgia
or both

TRYING NEW THINGS

my teeth scream
when i wake up
it's a new thing
    just started
    very cutting edge
    very chic
    very european or japanese
    (depending on where you're from)
could be a grind
maybe it's more of a clench
i wouldn't know
i'm not really there to see it
and i sleep alone

when i wake up
    the words are angrier than they were in the past
verbs clock me in the jaw
    because they're too beat to take action
    outside of a smattering of
    wham pow bang zaps
    fillings full of onomatopoeia
which
i mean
i get
i think we've all felt like that
    (wanting to punch me in the face)
now and again
but my dentist says i have to start
wearing some sort of mouthguard
    like a total nerd
    because even being unconscious is too rough on this
    delicate dweeb

DESTINATION SHRUG

soooooooooooo
where are we going
do we stay here
or
now that we are free
and fences have caught the plague
do we take off
run to the suburbs or farms
or wherever it costs less to live
are we allowed to run in the first place
do our jobs have legs
are we tethered to our paychecks and how long is the leash

i grew up in the country and it was common to see dogs
with leashes tied to clotheslines
(loosely)
so that they could run back and forth
but never get away
and the yards were wide open and without any other barriers
that's what the dream of not living in the city feels like
that's what dreaming of a world without landlords feels like
a sanctuary where
money and acceptance and safe spaces are plentiful

or do we stay put
because this is what we know
and it works even when it doesn't work

FROM: BEYOND

"you got this"
say the ghosts of
all of your ancestors
draped in hand me down quilts with eye holes cut out
hovering just far enough off the ground
to straddle the border of
scary and comforting

"you got this"
say the ghosts of
all of your ancestors
watching you struggle
to get out of bed
or brush your teeth
or put on pants
or keep it together

and sometimes they
take photos
on their cellphones
and text them to you
so that you can
make a scrapbook
of all of these momentous achievements
and call it
"a tribute to myself"

SHARING WALLS

pop quiz:
        what is my
        next door neighbour doing
this late
all the time
year round

what is the neighbour to the left of me
        (if you're facing my front door)
        (right if you're outside looking up from outside)
doing?
are they chiseling through the wall
        lonely in the isolation of the pandemic
the contemporary version of peeking over
a wooden fence that separates back yards
wilson would never

are they scratching from within the walls
is it even they
is it some nightmarish wraith
maybe where they come from
this is just the same as knocking
        they just want to borrow some sugar
and i'm the asshole for finding their approach so ghastly
and i'd rather this option than it be rats or mice

when the sounds aren't creepy
they're loud
consistently crystal clear
        a dj set
        a bunch of people
        (thanks for the invite)
        a banging the cupboards and a stomping walk
or laughs that can't not be forced

no one laughs that loud
i'm very funny
and nobody
has ever laughed that loud at one of my jokes
so if that's not scientific proof of an act
then i don't know what is

MARKETING RULES

they held my poems up
on the home shopping network
and said
        check out this dumb book full of dumb emotions
and said it
        with enthusiasm
        with a toothy mouth
        with a price and a phone number flashing

buy these weird feelings
that fell out of a swirling body
        tie dye thoughts
        whirlpool intestines
        spinning like a clear plastic bag
        with water and a live fish held by a kid on a bus
        or in the backseat of a car

relate
relate on installments
        if you can't afford it right now
relate and feel reassured
that you're not nuts
and if you are
then it is a common variety of nuts
community is a trust fall in the world of non-stop brains

FINAL RESTING FACE

i have found the most beautiful urn
for when I die
please scoop up ashtray me
and use this
wendy's baconator flavored pringles tube
to house the memory
and snow-like physicality
of me

the idea is hilarious to me
and if i can make my loved ones laugh
          make them roll their eyes
          or grin
from beyond the grave
then i think
it would be a nice way to say
          thank you for the crows feet
          and goodbye for now

be the poltergeist that you want to see in the world
dress for the job
that you want
          and not the
          goofy flesh prison
          that you're currently doing time in

GLOWING REVIEWS

i love showing my son
a new tattoo that i just got
then asking him if he likes it
knowing that he will look
            look pensive
            really put thought into it
and then say
            "not really"
every
single
time

CRYSTAL GAZING

the rainbow on my wall
        above the couch
        across my books
is too magical for atheism

i mean
i know about science
i've heard of it
i know about light
        and refractions
i know what made it
i bought the prism
        i stuck it to the window above the balcony door
but it's the feeling

it's the feeling that the rainbow gives me
        but more than anything
                gives my son
the special
the special is too magical
the wonder and excitement are too magical
the curiosity and double takes
        the make believe that he's pulled into
        thanks to something that i ordered off of the internet

some phone calls
        the ones you really look forward to
        because you don't get a voice with a text
are magical too
shooting the shit and making certain people laugh
that saving grace in a bullshit week

you too have probably experienced
a little bit of magic in recent times
(whether you were aware of the abracadabra or not)
something that fooled of frightened you
a hint of sorcery when everything blows
can go a long way
this is not sleight of hand
this is pure merlin
this is a flourish that i will always think of fondly

WELCOME BACK

all you want to do is go home
the headache is high beaming your brain
you're hungry
    or gassy
    or restless
    or too drunk
    or need to use the bathroom
    or you work tomorrow
    or you're surrounded by people but lonely

all you want to do is go home
that smell
    knowing where everything is
    knowing where everything used to be
    knowing how it works
    and where the light switches are
    and if the garbage can is in the cupboard under the sink
    and which cabinet the cups are in

all you want to do is go home
and sleep in that bed
    under those blankets
    and fall asleep on that couch
    while half-watching that show
    with that lamp on once it gets dark
    with food that only home has

all you want to do is go home
where everything is a bit warm and fuzzy
    even if the thermostat leans in the other direction
    and the bad guys can't get in
    because of the magic that homes have
    the safety in the insulation

and the photographs from before
in albums and frames
an impenetrable coziness
under popcorn ceilings

NO THANK YOU

i did a thing!
and i hated it
i mean
i guess the important thing is that i tried
that's the main thing right?
this thing
whatever it is
          i talked to somebody or left the house
          i bought a new style of pants
          i tried a new haircut

i'm open for change and experimentation!
i'm very modern and cultured!
i will never like the results,
but i'm open!
i'm willing to try stuff and know i won't like it
at the same time!
          (now that's multitasking baybay!)

but how do i know that i won't like the thing
          you ask
          (rudely)
because i have tried a lottttttt of thingsssssss
          possibly too many things
yes some are fine
          some are good
          some i like
but overwhelmingly
          if we really look at the data
          crunch numbers like sidewalk salt under winter boots
9 out of 10 scientists agree that i will
          "think it sucks"
that's like
          the technical term for my reaction

        (their words, not mine)
that's the baking powder making it with the vinegar
my response is the bubbly lava
        oozing out of the paper mâché volcano
        of my lived experiences

i'm sorry i got so highbrow for you
        not into science? you some sort of flat earther?

but i did a thing!
are you proud of me?
        can i stop doing new things now?
        can i just watch old kids in the hall episodes on repeat?
        is that what the award you're surely making me says?
        that it's time for a break?
        from new stuff
        from giving it a go
i can show you the research again
if you'd like
if that's what you're getting at
        i bought a printer just so you can take it all with you

i do really wish i could tell you
when the next big phase of me doing things is gonna be
        aaahhh!
my schedule is packed
and i'd need a lab
        maybe a grant
        who has time to write grants these days?
i've just got all these
        *gestures wildly at a recliner and tv
tasks that i have to complete
but the fact remains i did try something
and i may

(but won't)
try something else again in the not too distant future
(if you play your cards right)
thank you for your support

EVEN THE BOWLING ALLEY

it was called
the old concrete factory
even though it was probably younger than most of us
and it was still in use
        (probably not entirely made of concrete either)
but it felt old
maybe it was the dust
maybe it was our teenage
lack of understanding of how manual labor jobs
        ones with skills learned
        from parents and grandparents
        with gentle sandpaper hands
that made it seem old

and the grey
and the right angles of the big cement cubes
with hollowed out insides
        that looked designed to play manhunt around
and the open mouths of the big cement tubes
that we assumed were for sewers
        in the new subdivisions
        on the outskirts of towns
        because what else needs a huge pipe like that
and the sound the gravel ground made
as you walked around
        the tap dance of the unpaved

you couldn't visit during the day
because people were working
and we were busy with all of the things
young people in small towns in the 90s did
        vandalism and skateboarding
        and swearing and smoking
but at night we'd hop fences like commandos in action movies

crouch crawl up the shaft of an enclosed conveyor belt
        we didn't know what purpose it served
        other than making it easier to
        break into the attic of the main building
and then, through there, to the roof

it was the highest point in town and even looked down
        on the bowling alley
and we could see everything
        and we'd just lie there on the bumpy tar
        and it was pitch black above the streetlights
and all the corners of the town
spread out below us
        like a fitted sheet over a mattress that
        we all couldn't wait to leave
        but that was secretly providing us with
        the best sleeps of our lives.

ACKNOWLEDGMENTS

This book would not have been possible without the support of my family and friends. A special thank you to Henrik, my mom, Kerry & Jen, Stephanie and the Weinz family, Daniel Innes, Brent Orr, Filling Station, Poetry Is Dead, Chris and Now Or Never Publishing, Andrea, Bob, RC, Jason, everybody who has let me bounce ideas off of them or tuned into my virtual poetry readings while the world burns, used book stores, sertraline, professional wrestling, paranormal reality TV shows, and you for buying this book because that honestly means a lot. Thanks for being nice to me.